IF YOU WERE A
DOLPHIN

Clare Hibbert

W

FRANKLIN WATTS

LONDON • SYDNEY

First published in 2013 by Franklin Watts

Copyright © 2013 Arcturus Publishing Limited

Franklin Watts
338 Euston Road
London
NW1 3BH

Franklin Watts Australia
Level 17/207 Kent Street, Sydney, NSW 2000

Produced by Arcturus Publishing Limited,
26/27 Bickels Yard, 151–153 Bermondsey Street, London SE1 3HA

Editor: Joe Harris
Picture researcher: Clare Hibbert
Designer: Emma Randall

Picture credits:
All images Shutterstock unless otherwise specified. Corbis: 28tr. FLPA: 6tr, 7, 10r, 13 (main), 17t, 22, 23cr, 24tl, 26t, 26c, 27, 28bl.

A CIP catalogue record for this book is available from the British Library.

Dewey Decimal Classification Number: 597.9'6

ISBN: 978 1 4451 1874 1

Franklin Watts is a division of Hachette Children's Books, an Hachette UK company.
www.hachette.co.uk

Printed in China

SL002676EN
Supplier 03, Date 0513, Print Run 2369

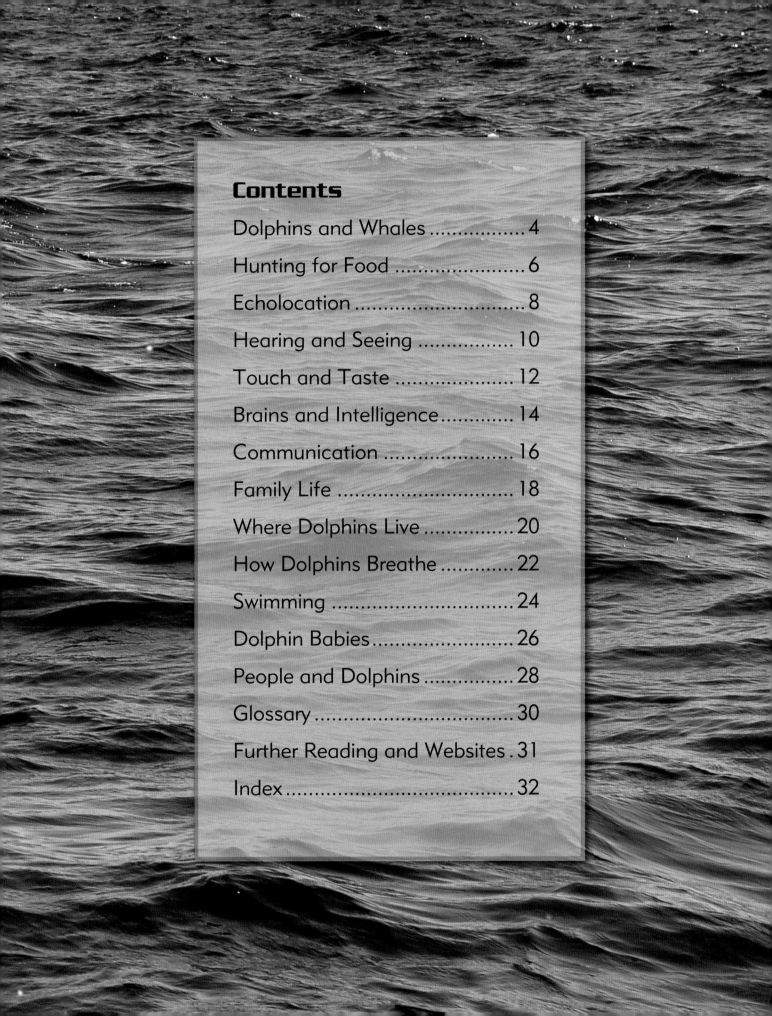

Contents

Dolphins and Whales

If you were a dolphin, you'd be a type of whale – a warm-blooded marine animal. You'd be a spectacular swimmer with a sleek, streamlined body. You'd also be intelligent, and able to communicate with other dolphins.

Toothed whales

The two main types of whale are whales with teeth and whales without teeth. Dolphins are toothed whales. Other toothed whales include sperm whales and belugas. Orcas, also known as killer whales, are a type of dolphin.

Dolphin Questions

Q: How many types of dolphin are there?
A: Experts cannot agree on an exact figure, but there are about forty. One problem is that not everyone agrees on which species are dolphins. Another is that some kinds are rare and dying out.

Toothless relatives

Whales without teeth are called baleen whales. Blue whales, humpback whales, right whales and grey whales are all baleen whales. They have bristly baleen instead of teeth, which they use to 'sieve' food from the water.

Small cousins

Porpoises are the smallest members of the whale family. They are only 1.5–2.5 m (5–8 ft) long. The harbour porpoise is the best-known. It is found in cool, coastal waters all over the northern hemisphere.

Hunting for Food

If you were a dolphin, you would be a carnivore, or meat-eater. You'd probably catch fish and squid to eat, or you might be a species that feeds on crustaceans. You might even be a fierce orca and hunt larger prey, such as baby seals and turtles.

Co-operating

Dolphins have some cunning hunting methods. They often team up to drive fish into a ball shape called a baitball. Other tricks include whacking fish with their tails to stun them or herding fish into the shallows.

Clever tricks

Dolphins use their brains when they are choosing where to hunt. They follow shrimp trawlers, for example, in order to pick off any fish attracted by all the shrimp. They even steal fish from fishers' nets.

Built for the job

Dolphins have wide, cone-shaped teeth, just right for grasping slippery prey. One set of between 60 and 100 teeth lasts them a lifetime. The teeth start coming through when baby dolphins are about five weeks old.

Dolphin Questions

Q: Which animals eat dolphins?
A: Sharks eat dolphins. Many dolphins have shark-bite scars on their bodies, so at least some of them get away. Orcas eat dolphins too – even though they belong to the same family.

Echolocation

If you were a dolphin, you would have a very special ability — echolocation. You'd be able to use sound to sense your surroundings, work out what objects and other living things were in the water with you, and navigate.

Using echolocation

Echolocation works by producing sounds and then listening for their echoes. Dolphins make high-pitched clicks that travel through the water. The clicking sounds bounce off objects, sending echoes back to the dolphins.

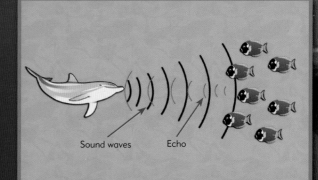

Sound waves   Echo

Pictures from sound

As they receive the echoes of the clicks, dolphins can build up a detailed picture of what is in the water. They can tell the exact shape and structure of things, and also how far away they are.

The melon

A dolphin's bulging forehead is a vital part of its echolocation equipment. The bulge is a fatty organ called the 'melon'. Its job is to direct or point the dolphin's clicks very precisely, so that the picture it builds up is as accurate as possible.

Dolphin Questions

Q: Can dolphins echolocate from birth?
A: Experts are still studying echolocation in newborn dolphins. They are fairly sure that calves are not born with the ability, but instead learn how to echolocate from their mothers.

Hearing and Seeing

If you were a dolphin, you wouldn't have ears on your head – you'd have internal (inside) ears only. You would probably have good eyesight, unless you were a river dolphin. You would be able to see in air, when you came up to look around, as well as underwater.

How dolphins hear

Sound travels as vibrations. Some sounds reach dolphins' internal ears through small openings just behind each eye. Most sounds, however, reach their ears by vibrating, or wobbling, along their lower jaws.

Eyesight

River dolphins usually have poor sight and rely on other senses, but most ocean-living dolphins see well. Like many animals, dolphins have a reflective mirror at the back of the eye, which helps them see better in dim or murky waters.

Spy-hopping

Dolphins often poke their heads above the surface to take a look around. This is called spy-hopping. They look out for big crowds of seabirds – a clue that there'll be plenty of fish in the water below.

Dolphin Questions

Q: Do dolphins cry?
A: Yes, dolphins' eyes 'weep' all the time. The oily tears keep the eyes clean – they're not a sign that the dolphins feel sad!

Touch and Taste

If you were a dolphin, touch would be one of your main senses. You'd use touch to find out more about the world, and to be friendly to other dolphins and people. You'd have smooth, sensitive skin. You would also have a sense of taste, which would help you to find food.

Feeling for prey

Dolphins have extra touch receptors on their flippers, so these are more sensitive than other parts of their bodies. Dolphins sometimes use their flippers to feel for crustaceans hidden in the sand of the seabed.

Touchy feely

Dolphins are very sociable and live in groups called pods. They touch each other when they are being friendly. They pat, stroke and nuzzle their friends with their flippers and snouts.

Dolphin Questions

Q: Can dolphins smell?
A: Dolphins have no smelling (olfactory) nerves, so they cannot smell at all. However, they can detect chemicals in the water using their taste buds.

Sense of taste

Dolphins have taste buds at the base of their tongue. Experts are still investigating dolphins' sense of taste, and we do not know very much about it. However, the animals certainly appear to prefer certain foods to others.

Brains and Intelligence

If you were a dolphin, you'd be very clever. The size of your brain in relation to your body would be about the same as a human being's. However, just because you had a big brain, it wouldn't mean you were quite as smart as a human.

Language

Humans are the only animals that use spoken language. However, researchers have shown that dolphins can learn sound-based language and sign language. The dolphins can even grasp how changing the order of words changes their meaning.

Being smart

Intelligence is about understanding, learning, solving problems and being creative. Dolphins are good at all of these things. However, their intelligence is not the main reason for their brain size. Experts think their extra-large brain is needed for echolocation.

Memory skills

Dolphins seem to have good memories. They can mimic sounds they've just heard, which shows that they have a good short-term memory. They also lay down long-term memories, and will remember animals, places or experiences for many years.

Dolphin Questions

Q: What else do dolphins have in common with us?
A: Dolphins can recognize their own reflections in a mirror. No other animals – apart from humans and chimpanzees – can do this!

Communication

If you were a dolphin, you'd have amazing communication skills. You'd use touch and body language to talk, but mostly you'd depend on sound. You'd produce an extraordinary range of different noises to let others know where you were and what you were up to.

Sound signals

Dolphins make all sorts of sounds when they are 'talking' to each other – squawks, whistles, squeaks, barks, groans and moans. Experts have even noticed that each dolphin group or pod has its own way of talking, like a 'dialect'.

Body language

Dolphins use body language to communicate too. A dolphin might roll over and 'play dead' to show that it is no threat to another dolphin. Or it may shake its head rapidly from side to side as a sign of aggression.

Dolphin Questions

Q: Do dolphins have names?
A: Dolphins often 'call out' the signature whistles of other dolphins. They are using the sounds like names to call their friends!

Whistles

Every dolphin has its own signature whistle to identify itself to other dolphins. Males adopt their mum's whistle, but females make up their own. How dolphins whistle seems to reveal their state of mind – whether they are feeling relaxed or fearful, for example.

Family Life

If you were a dolphin, you'd live in a close family group called a pod. There would probably be about a dozen of you. Sometimes, if you found a large amount of good food, your pod might join up with hundreds of other pods for a short time and be part of a huge super-pod.

What's in a pod?

Different dolphin species group together in different kinds of pod. Bottlenose dolphins often form groups of only females, or only females and calves. Dusky dolphins and white-beaked dolphins prefer to live in mixed pods that contain males, females and calves.

Caring dolphins

No one can say if dolphins feel emotions, but they definitely look after one another. Dolphins have been seen staying with ill or injured members of their pod, and saving their lives by nudging them up to the surface to breathe.

Loners

It's unusual for dolphins to live alone. Sometimes lone dolphins do show up in harbours and choose to live near humans. It may be that they've become separated from their pod, or are too old to keep up.

Dolphin Questions

Q: Do dolphins ever fight?

A: Yes. They're not always friendly! Male dolphins will fight rivals to win a mate – they fight by bashing each other with their tails.

Where Dolphins Live

If you were a dolphin, you might spend your life in rivers, but you'd be more likely to live in salty seas and oceans. Depending on your species, 'home' could be a warm, tropical sea, or chillier water closer to the poles.

Home ranges

Dolphins stick to their home ranges. Ocean species that live far away from the shore have the largest ranges, because their food is more spread out. For example, dusky dolphins range over 1,500 sq km (580 sq mi).

Adapted for their homes

Dolphins have a special kind of camouflage that makes them perfectly adapted to their watery habitat. Viewed from above, their darker backs are hard to spot against the watery depths. Viewed from below, their paler undersides blend in with the sunlit surface.

River dolphins

Several kinds of dolphin live in rivers. South America's great Amazon River is home to two types – tucuxi and botos. Many river dolphins are endangered. The Yangtze river dolphin recently became extinct because of pollution.

Dolphin Questions

Q: Do dolphins migrate?
A: Not really, though they might move into slightly warmer waters as the seasons change. They don't make regular long journeys like some of their whale cousins do.

How Dolphins Breathe

If you were a dolphin, you would swim like a fish, but you'd really be a warm-blooded mammal. Unlike a fish, you wouldn't be able to take in oxygen from the water. You'd need to breathe in air.

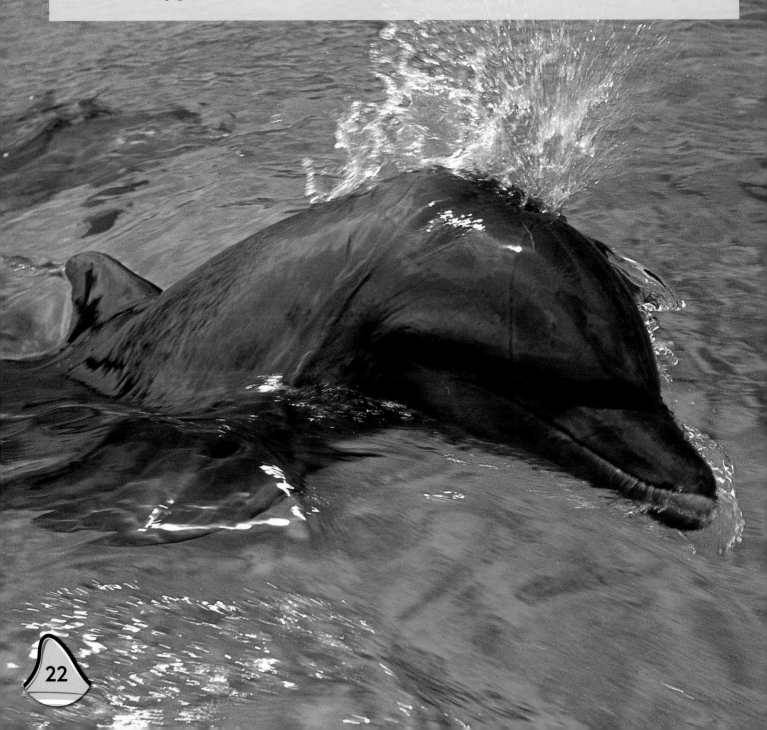

In and out

Dolphins come up to the surface to breathe. They take in air and get rid of waste gas through their blowhole, a hole on the top of their head. When dolphins are underwater, a flap covers the blowhole so water can't get in.

Big, blue blower

Dolphins and other toothed whales have one blowhole. The prize for the most impressive blow goes to the blue whale (pictured right). Its blowhole spray jets up to 12 m (40 ft) high – that's higher than a house.

Spray and bubbles

Dolphins sometimes spray water from their blowhole. This spray is water that was sitting on top of the blowhole. Once that's out of the way, the dolphin can breathe in and out – then dive under again.

Dolphin Questions

Q: How long can dolphins stay underwater?
A: It depends on their species and their age (older dolphins have bigger lungs). The longest is about 15 minutes. Dolphins slow down their heartbeat during a dive to reduce how much oxygen they use up.

Swimming

If you were a dolphin, you'd be perfectly at home in the sea. Your streamlined, smooth-skinned body would power you through the water. You'd be quite an acrobat, skipping and dancing just above the surface as you showed off your dizzying spins and turns.

Above the water

Dolphins are very playful – they often leap out of the water and even perform somersaults. Spinner dolphins are named for their habit of twisting and spinning in mid-air.

In the water

Dolphins swim by moving their muscular tails up and down. The upward movement, called the power stroke, is what pushes the animal through the water. Dolphins use their flippers to steer and turn.

Formation 'flying'

Dolphins swim close to their fellow pod members. Sometimes, a group of dolphins near the surface will make long, low leaps from the water as they swim along at speed – this is called porpoising.

Dolphin Questions

Q: How fast can dolphins swim?
A: Dolphins cruise along at 5–12 kph (3–7 mph), but speed up to chase prey. Orcas can swim at 55 kph (34 mph) in short bursts.

Dolphin Babies

If you were a dolphin, you would have started life as a calf. You'd have developed inside your mother for about a year before birth. Like all mammal babies, you would have fed on your mother's milk.

First moments

Most dolphin mothers give birth to a single calf – twins are very rare. The calf is born tail-first and can swim straight away. Its mother nudges it towards the surface to take its very first breath.

Family resemblance

Some dolphin babies look just like smaller versions of their parents – but not all. Spotted dolphin babies are born without spots (see left). The spots only begin to appear when the dolphins are about a year old.

Discipline

Youngsters that don't come when they're called or misbehave in some other way are told off with a tail slap. Any adult in the pod will care for or discipline the calves. Female 'aunties' babysit while the mothers hunt.

Dolphin Questions

Q:How long do calves stay with their mums?
A: Calves stick with their mums for at least two to three years, and sometimes for as long as six years.

People and Dolphins

If you were a dolphin, it's likely that you would meet people. You might swim with them, or you might be one of the dolphins that people keep in captivity. Even if you were free and wild, people's actions might threaten your survival.

Swimming with dolphins

Dolphins are a big tourist attraction in some parts of the world. People love watching them perform tricks, and they love swimming with them. Contact with dolphins can help children and adults with special needs, who may have difficulty communicating with others.

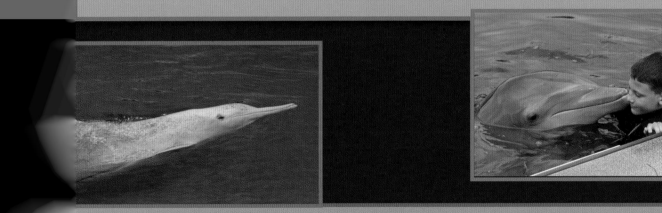

Threats to dolphins

Unfortunately, some human activities harm dolphins. Dolphins can get trapped in large fishing nets. Many, including the rare humpback dolphin (pictured), are threatened because of pollution, which damages their habitat and the fish they eat.

Dolphin superheroes

There are many true stories of gentle, friendly dolphins helping swimmers to escape from sharks and saving people's lives. Dolphins seem to be naturally kind and caring – not only to each other but to people too.

Dolphin Questions

Q: Can dolphins smile?
A: One reason why people find dolphins so appealing may be their 'smile'. It's not a real smile, though – it's just the way dolphins' mouths are structured.

Glossary

baitball A mass of fish prey that has been herded together into a ball.

baleen Bristly, comb-like plates that hang from the upper jaw of some whales, and that are used to sieve small items of food from the water.

blow The spray from a whale or dolphin's blowhole.

blowhole The 'nostril' on the top of a dolphin's head, through which it breathes in and out.

captivity Being confined and not free to get away. Some dolphins that perform in tourist resorts are born in captivity, but many are captured from the wild.

carnivore An animal that has a diet of mostly meat (or fish).

co-operating Working together to achieve a shared aim.

crustacean A creature with a hard shell, such as a crab or lobster. Most crustaceans live underwater.

echolocation A way of using sound to find food and to navigate. Dolphins make clicks and then listen to the returning echoes to work out what is around them.

endangered In danger of dying out.

extinct Describes an animal that has completely died out in the wild.

home range The area where an animal lives.

marine To do with or living in the sea.

melon The oval organ inside a dolphin's forehead that focuses its clicks to improve the accuracy of its echolocation.

migrate To make a regular, usually seasonal, journey from one place to another in search of food or a mate, or to give birth.

mimic Copy.

navigate To find the way.

northern hemisphere The half of the world that lies above the Equator (the imaginary line that goes around the middle of the Earth).

nuzzle Rub softly with the snout.

organ A body part that has a particular function.

pod A group of dolphins that live and hunt together.

pollution Damage to water, soil or air by poisonous substances.

porpoising Leaping out of the water and moving forwards at speed, usually as part of a group.

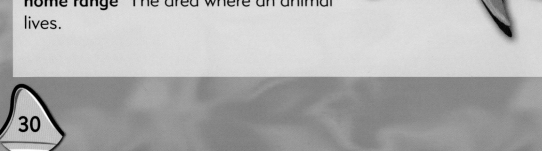

prey An animal that is hunted by other animals for food. Fish, squid and crustaceans are typical prey for dolphins.

receptor A part of the body that can sense, or receive information about, the surroundings.

rival A competitor. Male dolphins are often rivals, competing for the attention of females.

spy-hopping Raising the head above the surface of the water to see what is going on.

taste buds Receptors in the mouth that send signals to the brain, which then makes sense of that information allowing an animal to taste.

trawler A fishing boat that trails a large net to catch fish or other sea animals.

Further Reading

100 Facts: Whales and Dolphins by Steve Parker (Miles Kelly Publishing, 2008)

Everything Dolphins by Elizabeth Carney (National Geographic Society, 2012)

Infosearch: Dolphins by Anna Claybourne (Heinemann, 2005)

Sea Hunters: Dolphins, Whales and Seals by Andrew Solway (Heinemann, 2013)

Whales, Dolphins and Porpoises by Mark Cawardine (Dorling Kindersley, 2010)

Websites

kids.nationalgeographic.com/kids/animals/creaturefeature/bottlenose-dolphin/Information on Bottlenose dolphin facts and pictures

www.arkive.org/boto/inia-geoffrensis/
Information, photos and video of the endangered Amazon river dolphin, or boto

www.bbc.co.uk/nature/life/Cetacea
A BBC guide to whales, dolphins and porpoises that includes news stories and video footage

www.immersionlearning.org/index.php?option=com_wrapper&Itemid=87
An interactive guide to how dolphins communicate

www.wdcs.org.uk
The UK homepage for the Whale and Dolphin Conservation Society

Index

Series Contents

If You Were a Cat How Cats Hunt • Cats' Eyes • Amazing Senses • Contented Cats • Grumpy Cats • Body Language • The Home Range • How Cats Move • Caring for Fur • Cat Food • Kittens • Cat Breeds • Humans and Cats

If You Were a Dog Sight, Sound and Touch • A World of Smell • Chasing and Herding • Walkies! • Pack Animal • Dog 'Talk' • Body Language • Dog Feelings • Training • Meal Times • Care for Fur • Puppy Development • Humans and Dogs

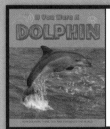

If You Were a Dolphin Dolphins and Whales • Hunting for Food • Echolocation • Hearing and Seeing • Touch and Taste • Brains and Intelligence • Communication • Family Life • Where Dolphins Live • How Dolphins Breathe • Swimming • Dolphin Babies • People and Dolphins

If You Were a Horse Horse Senses • Horse Eyes • Ears and Hearing • Body Language • Horse Talk • Friendship • Feeding • Grooming • Running Free • Resting • Mother and Foal • Working Horses • Horse and Rider

If You Were a Shark All Kinds of Shark • Shark Teeth • Sight and Sound • Smell, Taste and Touch • Super Senses • On the Move • Shark Tails • Maneaters • Pack Hunters • Filter Feeders • Migration • Shark Babies • A Very Strange Family

If You Were a Snake Seeing and Hearing • Super Senses • Hunting Tricks • Constrictors • Venomous Snakes • Feeding • How Snakes Move • Swimming Snakes • Snake Talk • Snake Defences • Snake Skin • Baby Snakes • Where Snakes Live